Festival Te Deum

founded on traditional themes

T0083169

©Oxford University Press 1937. Renewed in U.S.A. 1965. Printed in Great Britain
OXFORD UNIVERSITY PRESS, MUSIC DEPARTMENT, WALTON STREET, OXFORD OX2 6DP
Photocopying this copyright material is ILLEGAL.

All the earth doth wor - ship thee: the Fa - ther ev - er - last -
1
- ing.
1
ff
To thee all An - gels cry a - loud: the

Heav - ens, and all the Powers there - in.
2
sempre ff
To thee Cher-u - bin, and Ser - a -
sempre ff
2
-phin: con - tin-ual - ly do cry,

ff
Ho - - - ly, Ho - -
ff
ff
- ly, Ho - - ly: Lord God of
3
Sa - ba - oth; Heaven and earth are
3
ff

full: of the Ma - jes - ty of thy Glo -
-ry.
ff
4
f risoluto
The glo-ri-ous com-pa-ny of the A-pos-tles: praise thee;
f risoluto
4
f

The good-ly fel-low-ship of the Pro-phets: praise thee;
The no-ble ar-my of Mar - tyrs: praise
thee;
The ho-ly Church through -

- out all the world: doth ac -
- know - ledge thee;
5
ff
The Fa - ther: of an in - fi - nite Ma - jes - ty;
ff
5
ff

Thine hon - our-a - ble, true: and on-ly
Son; Al - so the Ho - ly Ghost: the
ff
6
Com - fort - er.
6
f dim.
con 8ves.

p
ff
ff
Thou art the King of Glo - ry:
ff
O
Christ.

7
Thou art the ev - er - last - ing Son: of the
7
poco più lento
Fa - - - ther.
poco più lento ♩ = 64
p
SOPRANOS ONLY
pp
When thou took - est up -
pp

-on thee to de - liv - er man: thou didst not ab-hor the Vir-gin's
8
womb.
p BASSES ONLY
When thou hadst o - ver - come the
8
pp
Tempo I
SOPRANO f risoluto
ALTO
thou didst o - pen the King-dom of
TENOR
BASS f risoluto
sharp-ness of death:
Tempo I
f marcato

heaven to all be -
- liev - - ers. Thou sit - test
at the right hand of God: in the

Glo - ry of the Fa - - ther.
9 rit.
poco meno mosso
ppALTOS ONLY
We be -
BASSES ONLY
pp
9 rit.
dim.
poco meno mosso
pp
- lieve that thou shalt come: to be our

Judge. We there - fore pray thee,
help thy ser - vants: whom thou hast re - deemed with
Tempo I
SOPRANO
p
cresc.
ALTO
thy pre - cious blood. Make them to be
TENOR
BASS
p
cresc.
Tempo I
p
cresc.

f
num-bered with thy Saints: in
f
simile
f
simile
10
ff
glo - ry ev - er - last - - ing,
ff
10
ff
in glo - ry ev - er -

- last - - ing, in
glo - ry ev-er - last - ing.
ff
11
f risoluto
O Lord, save thy peo - ple:
f risoluto
11
ff

and bless thine her - it - age.
ff
Gov - ern them: and lift them up for ev - er.
f
simile
ff
Day by day: we mag-ni - fy thee; And we
ff
ff

12
wor-ship thy name: ev-er world with-out end.
12
f
p
Vouch-safe, O Lord: to
p
dim.
p
keep us this day with-out sin. O Lord, have mer-cy up-on us:

pp
have mer - cy up - on us. O Lord, let thy mer - cy
pp
pp
dim. poco rit.
13
a tempo
light - en up - on us: as our trust is in thee.
dim.
poco rit.
13
a tempo
pp cresc.
ff risoluto
O Lord, in thee have I
ff risoluto
ff

Halstan & Co. Ltd., Amersham, Bucks., England

OXFORD UNIVERSITY PRESS